Till Eulenspiegel's
Merry Pranks
Op. 28

DATE

Richard Strauss

DOVER PUBLICATIONS, INC.
Mineola, New York

Dedicated to his dear friend Dr. Arthur Seidl

Till Eulenspiegel's Merry Pranks

Op. 28 (1894–5)

"After the old rogue's tale, set for large orchestra in rondo form"

•

INSTRUMENTATION

Piccolo [kl(eine) Fl(öte)]
3 Flutes [gr(osse) Fl(öten)]
3 Oboes [Ob(oen)]
English Horn [engl. Horn]
Clarinet in D [Clar(inette)]
2 Clarinets in B♭ ("B") [Clar(inetten)]
Bass Clarinet in B♭ ("B") [Bassclar(inette)]
3 Bassoons [Fag(otten)]
Contrabassoon [Contrafag(otte)]

4 Horns in F [Horn]
    (+ 4 Horns in D, *ad lib.*)
3 Trumpets in F [Tromp(etten)]
    (+ 3 Trumpets in D, *ad lib.*)
3 Trombones [Pos(aunen)]
Bass Tuba [Tuba]

Timpani [Pauken]

Percussion
    Triangle [Triangel]
    Cymbals [Becken]
    Bass Drum [gr(osse) Trom(mel)]
    Snare Drum [kl(eine) Trom(mel)]
    Large Rattle (Ratchet) [gr(osse) Ratsche]

Violins I, II [Violinen, Viol.]
Violas [Bratschen, Br.]
Cellos [Violoncelle, Vcl.]
Basses [Contrabässe, C.B.]

GLOSSARY OF GERMAN TERMS

alle, all of them play
allmählich lebhafter, gradually more lively
ausdrucksvoll, expressively

Becken allein, cymbals alone

Dämpfer weg, remove mutes
des, of the
des vorigen Zeitmasses, of the foregoing
 tempo
die eine Hälfte . . . die andere . . . , one half
 . . . , the other . . .
die Hälfte, only half of them play
die übrigen, the others
doppelt so langsam [schnell], twice as slow
 [fast]
drängend, urgently
dreifach, in three parts
drohend, threateningly
dumpf, muffled

entstellt, distorted
erste Solovioline, first solo violin
Erstes Zeitmass, first tempo
etwas breiter, somewhat more broadly
etwas gemächlicher, at a somewhat more
 comfortable tempo

gedämpft, muted
Gemächlich, comfortably paced
geschmeidig, with suppleness
gestopft, stopped notes
geteilt, divided
gleichgültig, with unconcern
grosse Trommel allein, bass drum alone

im Zeitmass des Anfangs, in the tempo
 of the beginning
immer (ausgelassener und) lebhafter, more
 and more (exuberant and) lively

Immer sehr lebhaft, continuing very lively

kläglich, mournfully

lang, long
leichtfertig, frivolously
liebeglühend, amorously
lustig, merrily

mit Dämpfern, with mutes
mit Holzschlägel(n), with (a) wooden
 stick(s)
mit Schwammschlägeln, with soft sticks

nicht eilen!, don't rush!
nicht geteilt, not divided

offen, open notes
ohne Dämpfer, without mutes

ruhig(er), (more) calmly

Saite, string
scharf gestossen, with sharp staccato
schelmisch, roguishly
schnell und schattenhaft, fast and shadowy
sehr lebhaft, very lively
Solobratsche, solo viola
steigern, more intensely

vierfach, in four parts
Volles Zeitmass, full tempo

wieder noch einmal so langsam, just that
 much slower again
wütend, furiously

zart, tenderly
zusamm(en), together
zweite Solovioline, second solo violins

Till Eulenspiegel's Merry Pranks
Op. 28

4

38

12

147

229

281

346

38

495

32

32

48

534

550
immer ausgelassener und lebhafter.
kl. Fl.
3 gr. Fl.
3 Ob.
engl. Horn.
Clar. (D)
2 Clar. (B)
Bassclar. (in B.)
3 Fag.
Contrafag.
4 Hörner. (in F.)
3 Tromp. (in F.)
3 Pos. Tuba.
Pauken.
f cresc.
ff
immer ausgelassener und lebhafter.
I. Viol. II.
Br.
Vcl.
C B.

558
37
kl. Fl.
3 gr. Fl.
3 Ob.
engl. Horn.
Clar.(D)
2 Clar.(B)
Bassclar. (in B.)
3 Fag.
Contrafag.
I. III.
4 Hörner (in F.)
II. IV.
I.
3 Tromp. (in F.)
II. III.
3 Pos.
Tuba.
Pauken.
(mit Holzschlägeln)
I.
Viol.
II.
Br.
Vcl.
C B.
ff

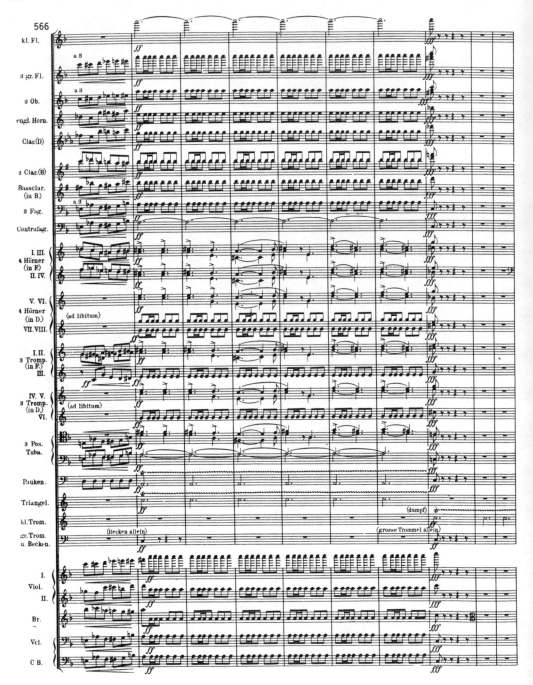

München, 6. Mai 1895.

END OF EDITION

A00001302677